STEAM
ON
SHED

STEAM
ON
SHED

JOHN STRETTON

CHANCELLOR
PRESS

First published in the UK 1984 by Blandford Press,
Link House, West Street,
Poole, Dorset, BH15 1LL

This edition published 2003 by Chancellor Press,
an imprint of Bounty Books, a division of
Octopus Publishing Group Limited,
2-4 Heron Quays, London E14 4JP

A CIP catalogue record for this book is available from the British Library

ISBN 0 7537 0755 1

Typesetting and design by Weaver & Associates, Weymouth, Dorset, England

Printed and bound in Italy

FOREWORD

My first memory of a shed visit, is of reaching Mansfield shed in the pouring rain, on a trip organized by the Nottingham-based Attenborough Model Railway Society. Collecting the engine numbers in the shed yard, in the rain, was difficult enough, but was just as arduous inside the buildings, as the shed had definitely seen better days and was more sky than roof! My first photo visit, was to Leicester Midland one Sunday morning, with David Richards (one of the contributors to this book) and another friend, in the late 50s. Both of these were in the very early days of my train-spotting career, before I had really begun to realise the set-up of the railway network, or to appreciate the bewildering variety of engines around, or the enormity of my ambition to 'spot' them all! When, by 1960, I had fully taken in the railway facts of life, building of steam had finished, diesels were beginning to appear and what had seemed so permanent, sometimes disappeared overnight. The race was on to see and photograph as much of steam as was possible, within the constraints of time and money, before it all vanished completely.

In those years 1960-68, the experiences and memories became legion. As knowledge of BR locos increased, so did the yearning to complete classes, to see all the locos of a particular type; to do this, meant visiting as many of the sheds as possible, the length and breadth of the country. Inevitably, organized tours seemed to miss the particular venues in which I was interested, so I started my own train-spotting club — purely so I could choose which sheds to visit! On top of this, of course, one made solo forays throughout the country. One such was a train trip from Leicester to Liverpool (itself a great pleasure, over the now non-existent Midland main line from Derby to Manchester), to visit Bank Hall shed. I'd heard that 'Jubilee' No. 45719 *Glorious* was out of action on shed and it was my last want of the class. The great problem was — no permit. Memory has it that, trying the brazen way in, I was summarily ejected by the foreman. Unfortunately, past his office was the only way in — there was no back way; so how to get in? Hanging about outside, a Scouse railman, about to go in and sign on, guessed my plight and offered help. Advising me to walk close behind him, he marched up to the foreman's window and then stood there as a shield, while I crouch-ran, Red Indian-style, to the door and the steps down into the shed proper. My antics would have graced a silent movie, but were worth it, as *Glorious* was indeed on shed, at the back, looking a very sorry sight. My joy was full, but then tempered by the thought that I had to get out again. That walk back up the stairs, through the door at the top, past the office and out into the street, was one of the longest I have ever taken and I was convinced that I was to be discovered, or have my heart stop, at every step. A fortnight later, I took our club to the shed – *Glorious* was gone!

Another memory of the Lancashire area, is of 27D (Wigan L & Y). Arriving there in the evening, having been touring sheds in the area all day, the sun had passed throwing long shadows and it was becoming difficult to see the numbers of the engines standing in the yard. This was nothing, however, to the situation inside the shed. There were lights, or I think there were! The smog inside the buildings would have done credit to Los Angeles on its worst day; all the engines must have been in full steam all day and there must have been some fault in the ventilation system, as a green pall hung down from the ceiling to about waist height. Not only was it nigh on impossible to see the cab side numbers, but the fog was blinding and choking and, as we emerged from the shed, trying to find the sanctuary of our coach, we all looked and coughed as though we had been victims of a gas attack! On another day, the coach was again a haven, as we were chased from Birkenhead shed buildings – not by an irate foreman, but by 7/8-year old kids hurling half-house-bricks.

The fear of the shed foreman, mentioned above, was ever present, even if he had given permission to tour his depot; but if he hadn't, the adrenalin really flowed.

There was not a lot we could do, however, at Goole. We arrived at the end of our long walk to the shed, to be met by a very angry foreman at the head of the yard, arms crossed. He would not be pacified by the fact that we had a permit – his main concern was that, the day before our visit, a diesel had been set afire, on shed, by other 'enthusiasts'. Not surprisingly, he was not kindly disposed towards train-spotters. He did, however, allow one of our party to take the numbers of the engines that we could see in the yard – hence the details to the photograph in this book. Cardiff East Dock and Banbury also said 'no' – but with stealth that would have done real credit to the mythical Red Indian, we managed to get our party of 30-odd teenagers round, record all the numbers and manage to take the odd photograph!

By contrast, the foreman at Leicester Midland was most understanding. As I worked in Leicester, he had agreed that I could tour the shed daily at lunch time, without asking his permission each time. This arrangement worked wonderfully for a couple of weeks – until I was caught one lunch by the Inspector. He was not at all amused by the arrangement. A policeman at Crewe South, thought he had a friend and myself 'cold', when he caught us on shed, right at the end of steam there. He was genuinely amazed when I produced our permit – he had not seen an official spotter for over 6 months. And Crewe North shed once displayed physical evidence of the risk one took when 'bunking' sheds – impaled on the rusty spike of the shed fencing, was the end of a finger – obviously, one spotter had left in very much of a hurry. When I saw it, it was long since white – presumably left there as a warning!

On a lighter note, visits could bring forth the unexpected. If you were lucky, a kind driver would give you rides round the yard; you could discover an engine way off its beaten track, like the time I saw a 'B1' on Redhill; or you could witness some event, like the 'Black 5' I saw back into a siding at Carnforth, its crew get out and its final move over, it was left to die!

Such are the stuff of memories – but sheds were not there for our benefit.

Motive Power Depots were around from the earliest days, but really developed from the 1860s on, when it was felt by the various railway authorities, that there was a need for buildings where the engines could be under cover, out of the damaging effects of the elements; repairs could be carried out on the engines, in relative peace and comfort; and there could be, incorporated into the buildings complex, facilities for the staff, a central control point and a permanent place for the engine records.

As the sheds grew out of the needs of the area and the individual sites, they were all unique. There would be common factors, but no two would be identical. For the enthusiast, this made a visit yet more enjoyable, for there would always be a special something that would make the visit memorable. And for photographers, this very uniqueness opened the door for an unending variety of shots, angles, etc.

The atmosphere of a steam shed, is something that lingers in the memory. Even now, years later, an odd vision, caught out of the corner of the eye, or a certain smell, will bring it all flooding back, with all its attendant nuance of memory. It is an atmosphere that is virtually impossible to fully encapsulate in words and photographers have tried, as long as there have been cameras, to capture the very spirit of a shed scene.

It may be the smoke drifting lazily across a shed yard, as engines stand in warm summer sun; it may be the far more forlorn sight of engines standing, like disgraced dogs, in the pouring rain; there are the myriad patterns, as sunshine shafts through the shed roofs; there were the shots of workmen carrying out running repairs; or the expectant bustle, as an engine and crew prepared to leave the shed confines, for their next duty; there was the surprise sighting; or the juxtaposition of the strange and the familiar; there was the large and the small, young and old, cheek-by-jowl. And there was the dirt.

The steam engine was essentially a dirty beast and yet this very dirt was part of the charm and charisma of the animal. It made it look as though it worked hard and, occasionally, steam leaks evidenced that parts had, indeed, worked hard and were wearing out. For the railway photographer, it was these factors, more than any other, that attracted. Today's diesels and electrics have sharpened the photographic eye; with steam, there wasn't quite the same need, but, contrarily, we were almost spoilt for choice. At every turn, it seemed, there was a view, or sight, worth capturing. Thus, steam sheds, right up to their demise in 1968, had an appeal and an aura all their own. No amount of effort on the part of preservation societies, to recreate the scenes, can be successful – and excellent though some of these, like Didcot, Southall or Carnforth, are – as they are 'artificial'. Parts of these present sites capture moments – but nothing can recapture the entirety of the experience of a shed visit.

We have attempted, in the photos chosen for this book, to recapture as much of the essence of the appeal as we can. Steam sheds were not the cleanest of places and the sun didn't always shine and, hence, not all the photos in this collection are 'colourful'. Many show engines in less than pristine condition, but they have been purposely chosen, to show as many of the differing moods, aspects and lure of the sheds as possible. The pictures are all from the collections of myself, David Richards and Hugh Ramsey – all avid enthusiasts since the 50s and all wishing we could recreate what we all once took for granted. The book is basically in numerical order of shed codes from around 1960 and the numbers after each photograph, are: First, the number of engines allocated in 1950 and, second, the photographer: 1 – myself; 1L – from my collection, but taken by Les Wade; 2 – by Hugh Ramsey, and 3, by David Richards.

This, then, is Steam On Shed.

JOHN STRETTON

JANUARY 1984

Dedication
To Horace and Lucy – one for trying to put me off
and the other for making the sandwiches.

Plate 1: **1A WILLESDEN** On any trip to London, a visit to Willesden was imperative, both because it was close to Old Oak Common shed and because of the number and variety of engines to be seen. Here, on 19th July 1964, 'Coronation Pacific' No. 46240 *City of Coventry* looks good in her red livery, awaiting her next duty.   135;*1*

Plate 2: **1B CAMDEN** A mere three months on from the previous picture and *City of Coventry* has been withdrawn and stands ragged and a little forlorn, at the side of Camden shed buildings.   56;*1*

Plate 3: **2A RUGBY** With the Testing Station, the Great Central crossing the main line and numerous branch lines radiating from the town, Rugby was something of a train-spotting centre and the shed was always well worth a visit. A creditably clean 'Jubilee' No. 45629 *Straits Settlements,* is guest in late August 1961.   98;*1*

Plate 4: **2B NUNEATON** Even in electric days, Nuneaton managed to house a good number of steam engines of all shapes and sizes, and it did not actually close until 6th June 1966. More than two years earlier, on 5th April 1964, 'Jubilee' No. 45703 *Thunderer* stands proudly in the yard – she was withdrawn just seven months later. 73:1

Plate 5: **5B CREWE SOUTH** In early days, South shed languished in the shadow of the more glamorous North shed, but South stayed open to steam two and a half years after its neighbour. On 3rd September 1967, two months before closure, it housed 70 steam and 37 diesel engines, including 'Britannias' No. 70024 *Vulcan* and No. 70049 *Solway Firth* and 2-8-0 No. 48729.   103:1

Plate 6: **5B CREWE SOUTH** Another view on 3rd September 1967, typifying the freight emphasis of the shed. Seen, among others, are 2-8-0s Nos. 48522 and 48725 and 'Mogul' No. 43001.   *1*

Plate 7: **5A CREWE NORTH** Showing some of her size and power, 'Coronation' 4-6-2 No. 46224 *Princess Alexandra* simmers quietly under the coaling plant, on 16th April 1961.   85;2

Plate 8: **5A CREWE NORTH** Looking very smart, in contrast to her surroundings, 'Jubilee' No. 45567 *South Australia* stands patiently waiting her next call. Evidence can be seen of the cold wind and recent rain, on this dull March day in 1962.   3

Plate 9: **5A SUB-GRESTY LANE** The small sub-shed at Gresty Lane, gave house to the Western Region engines working into Crewe from Wales. Having just commuted from the South shed, Ivatt 2-6-2T No. 41241 stands in the company of 'Grange' No. 6848 *Toddington Grange.* 30th September 1962.   *1L*

Plate 10: **5D STOKE** Sunny days seemed to be the exception when 'shed-bashing'! Here, to illustrate the point, Standard Class 4 4-6-0 No. 75052 and 2-8-0 No. 48110 stand in the pouring rain. 3rd September 1967.   *99;1*

Plate 11: **6A CHESTER** The weather is no better here, but 'Jinty' No. 47507 doesn't seem to care, as she shunts other locos around the shed yard; and the locos on shed seem ready to add to the mirky conditions! Seen on 22nd August 1966, No. 47507 was withdrawn a week later.   38;3

Plate 12: **8B WARRINGTON** MR Class 5 No. 44934 seems in conversation with the Mini, inside Warrington shed, perhaps speculating on how long it is to the cutter's torch, as, on 7th October 1967, she is already withdrawn.   59;*1*

Plate 13: **8C SPEKE JUNCTION** The first months of 1963 saw some of the worst weather of the decade, with snow drifts common. Looking as cold as it undoubtedly was, 2-8-0 No. 48294 stands in the shed yard, seemingly having escaped the snow herself, in February of that year.   49;*3*

Plate 14: **8E NORTHWICH** Now used by preserved steam, in BR steam days it was home largely to freight engines. Here, Standard '9F' 2-10-0 No. 92166 is seen from inside the shed, enjoying the sunshine, in company with 2-8-0 No. 48151. 7th October 1967.   42:1

Plate 15: **8F SPRINGS BRANCH, WIGAN** Not a favourite shed on spotting tours, it always repaid a visit and, although thick with grime, 'Black 5' 4-6-0 No. 45145 still looks impressive in the bright sunshine of 7th October 1967. 57;1

Plate 16: **9A LONGSIGHT** Looking resplendent in the sunshine, 'Britannia' No. 70052 *Firth of Tay* is an obvious candidate for the camera. Shedded at Crewe North, and soon to be shipped further north, she was still fighting the electrics at this time. 28th March 1965.   129;*1*

Plate 17: **9B STOCKPORT** Positioned just to the south of Manchester city centre, Stockport shed always had a fascinating variety of engines present and, usually, they were well looked after. 'Black 5' No. 45279 seems to have benefited from an oily rag. 28th March 1965.   27;*1*

Plates 18 & 19: **9D BUXTON** Two views separated by three years. **(Above)** An unidentified 'Super D' 0-8-0 stands in the company of Nos. 42370 and 43213, in the sunshine of 4th August 1962, while three railmen enjoy their sandwiches. 55;2 **(Below)** In the evening sunshine of 28th March 1965, there seems to have been a funnel thief about, as Rebuilt 'Patriot' No. 45522 *Prestatyn* and 0-6-0 No. 44425 are without theirs! *1*

Plate 20: **9E TRAFFORD PARK** Resting inside the shed, 'Mogul' No. 43033 is covered with a layer of grey dust but otherwise is in good condition, in company with 'Jubilee' No. 45633 *Aden,* on 21st April 1963.   72;*1*

Plate 21: **9F HEATON MERSEY** Judging by the pile of brake blocks in the foreground, Heaton Mersey's drivers were heavy on the brakes! Whether 'Mogul' No. 43042 and 2-8-0 No. 48273 were the culprits is unknown, as they stand bathed in sunbeams on 28th March 1965. 63;*1*

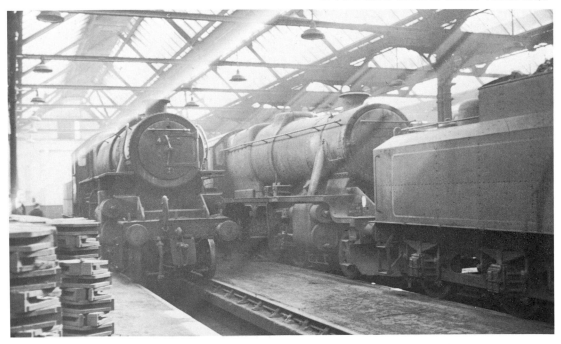

Plate 22: **9G GORTON** A general view of the shed yard, on 28th March 1965, showing, among others, 'Crab' No. 42700 and Fowler 2-6-4T No. 42369. 161;1

Plate 23: **9G GORTON** In 1950 the allocation was totally of Eastern engines and MR locos would have been a rarity; by 1965, however, they were the rule and original 'Crab' No. 42700 was not in the least out of place. 3

Plate 24: **12A CARLISLE KINGMOOR** Early morning activity on 22nd August 1964. In 1950, the most glamorous engine that the shed could boast was a 'Jubilee'; but by 1964, following their exile north, after the electrification through Crewe, the allocation of 'Coronations' was commonplace. No. 46257 *City of Salford* awaits further duties, with 'Mogul' No. 43103 as companion.   1

Plate 25: **12A CARLISLE KINGMOOR**
There is plenty of activity in evidence, north
of the shed, as 'Jubilee' No. 45626
Seychelles watches one of her sisters
leave the shed buildings.   *1*

Plate 26: **12A CARLISLE KINGMOOR**
Both 'Clan' No. 72005 *Clan Macgregor*
and 'Black 5' No. 44824 look raring to go,
as they stand in company, facing
south.   141;*1*

Plate 27: **12B CARLISLE UPPERBY** The late evening sun looks about to be covered by cloud, as 'Britannias' No. 70048 *Territorial Army 1908-58* and No. 70029 *Shooting Star* rest on shed, after working a train, double-headed, into Carlisle. 28th November 1964.   87;*3*

Plate 28: **12C CARLISLE CANAL** Canal shed was ever the Cinderella of Carlisle sheds and was the first to close in the 1960s. In the early 1950s its allocation was almost exclusively Eastern, including 'A3's and it remained a haven for such engines working cross-country from Newcastle, etc., until the end. Here, 'V2' No. 60900 looks in need of a clean, on Monday 6th August 1962.   58;*2*

Plate 29: **12E BARROW** The appearance of – left to right – Fowler 2-6-4T No. 42340, Stanier 2-6-2Ts Nos. 40081 and 40206 and Fowler No. 42402, tells the whole story – they are withdrawn. The last one spent the whole of her BR life at Barrow, presumably with low mileage! 50:2

Plate 30: **12H TEBAY** This pleasant, tranquil scene has been destroyed by the M6 Motorway, passing within yards of the shed! On 6th August 1962, however, peace reigns, as Fowler 2-6-4T No. 42414. is viewed from the coaler. She has companions on shed. but they are all very shyly hiding under cover! 10;2

Plate 31: **14A CRICKLEWOOD** The time is 1956, steam rules and Standard '9F' 2-10-0s are taking over from Garretts and '8F's on the Toton-Brent freights. Toton's No. 92065 stands in company with Crosti-boilered No. 92027 of Wellingborough, still in original condition, on 28th April, making a fascinating comparison.   89;2

Plate 32: **14A CRICKLEWOOD** Always predominantly a freight shed, eight years on from *Plate 31* and express engines were more common. 'Britannia' No. 70020 *Mercury* is still an unusual visitor, however, having arrived from Willesden, for attention, on 19th July 1964.   *1*

Plate 33. **14B KENTISH TOWN** The 'town' had the allocation for handling the Midland main line expresses out of St. Pancras and this allocation included a fair smattering of 'Black 5's. Visiting from Holbeck shed, No. 44853 looks in really fine condition, on 11th February 1962.   116;2

Plate 34: **14D NEASDEN** ER 'B16/3' No. 61472 is a real stranger in Neasden – allocated to York, she had worked down the Great Central main line on a Dundee-Marylebone 'extra' and is seen on shed, on Saturday, 20th July 1957.   81;2

Plate 35: **14D NEASDEN** Cup Final Day always brought a host of strangers to Neasden in steam days. The working is unknown that brought Standard Class 4 2-6-0 No. 76042 on shed, but the date is 5th May 1956.   2

Plate 36: **15C LEICESTER MIDLAND** Today the coaling plants no longer exist, nor any of the buildings behind, but otherwise, little has changed from this 1965 view of 'Jubilee' No. 45626 *Seychelles.* She rests on shed, waiting to return north, having worked a Saga Holidays Leeds–Eastbourne Special into Leicester.   80;*3*

Plate 37: **15C LEICESTER MIDLAND** Leicester's allocation, was almost exclusively workhorses and any special interest was from visitors. Standard '9F' 2-10-0 No. 92121 is a visitor, on 8th September 1965, seen amid some of the then current diesel workhorse allocation.   *3*

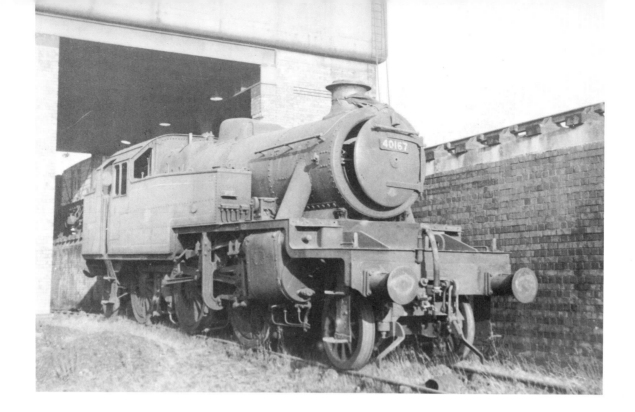

Plate 38: **15E LEICESTER CENTRAL** The shed once boasted 'A3's and named 'B1's, but with the transfer to MR control, the glamour quickly disappeared and Stanier 2-6-2T No. 40167 – one of only four with a large boiler – epitomizes the sense of anti-climax. Withdrawn in October 1961, she stands forlorn on Sunday, 14th January 1962.   *23;2*

Plate 39: **15E LEICESTER CENTRAL** English Electric gas turbine loco No. GT3, briefly brought a touch of glamour back to the Central in 1961. In light brown livery, touched out with dark green lining, she arrived in Leicester on 16th May 1961, straight from an exhibition at Marylebone. She is seen under the crane, on 21st May, immediately before running a diagram that took her to Marylebone twice daily.   *1L*

Plate 40: **16B KIRKBY-IN-ASHFIELD** In 1950, the allocation was largely Stanier 8F 2-8-0s; on 6th March 1966, it can be seen that not much has changed, although diesels are beginning to appear. Nos. 48621, 48362 and 48225. appear. Nos. 48003 and D1831 stand in company with Nos. 48621, 48362 and 48225. 62:1

Plate 41: **16D ANNESLEY** Rather like Leicester Central, Annesley was affected by transfer to MR control, but, on 29th July 1962, ER '01' 2-8-0 No. 63578 still gives the place a very Eastern air.   76;2

Plate 42: **17A DERBY** With the Midland's Works on site, Derby shed was a veritable mecca for spotters. Inside the roundhouse, on 20th October 1962, 'Jinty' No. 47320 looks diminutive beside '8F' Nos. 48336 and 48351, but all are healthily in steam. 136;2

Plate 43: **17A DERBY** Seen in the shed yard, on Sunday 16th October 1962, Johnson 3F 0-6-0 No. 43658 looks in fine shape; she has spent all her BR days at Derby, but has less than a year to live. This is an excellent shot for modellers.   *2*

Plate 44: **17A DERBY** Inside the round-house again, on 20th October 1962, the companions this time are Fairburn 2-6-4T No. 42161, Standard Class 2 No. 78028 and 'Black 5' No. 45407 (now of Carnforth).   *2*

Plate 45: **18A TOTON** The scene has changed radically since steam days at Toton and the signal box no longer exists, nor do the watering facilities. '4F' 0-6-0 No. 44376 is oblivious to all this, on shed on 14th January 1962, temporarily out of steam.   156;2

Plate 46: **21B BESCOT** Bescot closed to steam in March 1966, but eight months earlier, the picture still looked healthy. '4F' No. 44139 and '8F' No. 48101 stand with Nos. 44210, 48375, 48368, 46445, 43002, 48724, 76088, 46421, 48392 and 48769. 25th July 1965. 67;1

Plate 47: **21C BUSHBURY** This was a strange shed. Stuck in the wilds of northern Wolverhampton, it had to cope with virtually all Midland movement around the city and, consequently, had an amazingly mixed allocation. When seen on 1st December 1962, few LNWR 0-8-0s remained, but No. 48895 survived a further two years, despite the apparent steam leak! 41;1

Plate 48: **24B ROSE GROVE** Unglamorous the shed may have been, but it was one of the three to last to the end of steam. This was the scene just two days before the end, on 3rd August 1968, with '8F' 2-8-0 No. 48393 being admired, as one of the last in steam. 50:1

Plate 49: **24B ROSE GROVE** '8F' 2-8-0
No. 48024 looks almost shy, as she pokes
out from the shed buildings, but she will
not work again, being withdrawn shortly
after this photograph was taken, on 8th
October 1967. *1*

Plate 50: **24C LOSTOCK HALL** For the
very last day of working steam, Lostock
Hall worked hard at making the engines
presentable. Their success can be seen
from the condition of 'Britannia' No.
70013 *Oliver Cromwell* and 'Black 5' No.
45110. 4th August 1968. *43;1*

Plate 51: **24C LOSTOCK HALL** Another view of the final days of BR steam. The influx of diesels is readily visible, on 3rd August 1968, but steam is fighting to the last, in the form of 'Black 5's Nos. 44713 and 44942.   1

Plate 52: **24D LOWER DARWEN** The four named 'Black 5's were relative rarities and seemed shy of being photographed, but No. 45154 *Lanarkshire Yeomanry* is here captured in full glory, on 9th June 1963.   37;*1*

Plate 53: **24E BLACKPOOL (NORTH)** The South shed was actually the main one in Blackpool, but was the first to succumb to closure, with the North lasting until close to the end of steam. On 15th April 1968, there were actually 12 engines on shed, but they are not much in evidence around 'Black 5' No. 44690.   61 (between both sheds);*3*

Plate 54: **24E BLACKPOOL (NORTH)**
Another view of North shed, but this time with more people about and famous railway visitors. Midland Compound No. 1000 and 'A4' No. 60022 *Mallard* had not actually worked a train together, but had met up on shed, the latter having worked a special from Retford. 30th September 1961. *2*

Plate 55: **24H HELLIFIELD** Once a busy junction, Hellifield is now a skeleton, with only its station – a listed building – a reminder of its former glory, the shed buildings all gone. In happier days, there is ample activity, as MR '4F' 0-6-0 No. 43999 heads south on a freight, past 'Crab' No. 42813. 5th August 1961. *23;2*

Plate 56: **24L CARNFORTH** In latter days, Carnforth shed was host to withdrawn locos at the footpath entrance to the shed. A group can be seen in the background (with the funnel thief having struck again!) as 'Black 5' No. 45342 simmers quietly in the afternoon sun of 15th April 1968.
42:1

Plate 57: **26A NEWTON HEATH** Newton Heath was a big shed, with, in 1951, the seventh largest allocation in the country. Its range of engines covered the whole spectrum, but a good number were for local passenger services. Ivatt Class 2 2-6-0 No. 46485 (with increased cylinders) still fitted this bill on 28th March 1965, when she appeared not long out of works.   *167:1*

Plate 58: **26C BOLTON** The bane of a spotter's life was rain and the misery of it can well be judged from this view, from inside the shed, of Standard Class 5 4-6-0 No. 73069, standing in the pouring rain, on 5th November 1967. Bolton was another repository for withdrawn locos, as can be seen by those in the background. *47;1*

Plate 59: **26D BURY** Sunday, 9th June 1963, was a hot sunny day (making up for the previous winter!) A lethargy often seemed to settle on sheds in this heat and 'Austerity' 2-8-0 No. 90555 appears to be subject to it. *28;1*

Plate 60: **26E LEES (OLDHAM)** As can be seen, the shed building is modern, though the depot itself was much older. Its function was freight and local passenger and this was so until closure in May 1964. In June of the previous year, the lion's share of space is taken by 'Austerity' class locos.   25;*1*

Plate 61: **26F PATRICROFT** Finally closing on 1st July 1968, Patricroft was another largish shed serving Manchester and, again, it had a wide spectrum of locos. Standard Class 3 2-6-2Ts came late in the day and the original, No. 82000, has already lost her number-plate, a couple of months before withdrawal.   73;*3*

Plate 62: **26F PATRICROFT** Access to the shed area was gained by a footbridge over the main line and this gave a full view of the shed's near T-shape. This can well be seen from this view, taken on 28th March 1965.   *1*

Plate 63: **30A STRATFORD** Of all steam sheds, Stratford was by far the biggest, stretching over many acres and with an allocation almost doubling its nearest rival. One could expect to see almost any engine from the Eastern Region and, often, it housed strangers. 'J15' 0-6-0 No. 65460 is no stranger, being a Stratford engine and looks in immaculate condition, on 7th July 1962 — sadly, she was withdrawn just two months later!   *383;2*

Plate 64: **30A STRATFORD** A typical
scene inside a steam shed – rows of
engines, some under attention and the
occasional workman moving among them.
And on Sunday, peace and tranquillity also
set in. On Sunday, 26th March 1961,
'N7/3' No. 69713 and 'B1' No. 61233
head their respective rows; the latter ended
her days as a stationary boiler at March.   *2*

Plate 65: **30A STRATFORD** Outside the
shed, also on 26th March 1961, the sun
shines brightly and enjoying this and the
rest, is 'J50/2' No. 68924, but she has
just been withdrawn and will work no
more.   *2*

Plate 66: **31B MARCH** March was a long trek from anywhere, but was always worth a visit. Variety was assured and in their early days on the ER, 'Britannias' were common visitors. No. 70030 *William Wordsworth* is actually in store here, awaiting transfer to MR, in company with last-numbered 'J20' No. 64699, 'J20' No. 64699, 'J17' No. 65582 and sister 'J20' No. 64691 – all already withdrawn nine months   161:7L

Plate 67: **34A KING'S CROSS** In company with Old Oak Common, Stratford, Nine Elms and Willesden, King's Cross was a must to visit as a spotter and, especially, the Top shed. Here, crack ER express engines were stabled and pampered. Enough to bring joy to the heart of any steam lover, is the sight of clean 'A4's, side by side. No. 60014 *Silver Link* and No. 60003 *Andrew K. McCosh,* seem ready to do battle with 'Deltic' No. D9007, rather overshadowing 'B1' No. 61394. 11th February 1961.   160;2

Plate 68: **34A KING'S CROSS** Another view of that same 'Deltic', this time with 'A3' No. 60056 *Centenary,* determined to show she's ready for work.   2

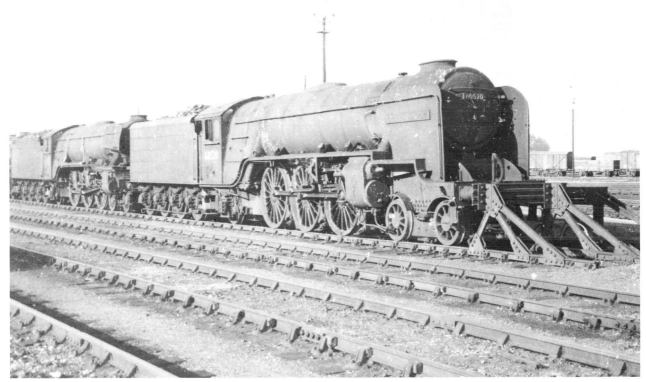

Plate 69: **34E NEW ENGLAND** At the time of this photograph, there were mass withdrawals of steam engines. In New England's yards, on 25th July 1963, 19 ER 'Pacifics' lay discarded, including eight 'A4's. Here, in perfectly serviceable condition, is 'A2/3' No. 60520 *Owen Tudor* and just behind, is 'A3' No. 60050 *Persimmon* – thus ended the reign of New England as the third largest allocation in Britain. 213;1L

Plate 70: **34F GRANTHAM** Grantham, of course, was the staging post of East Coast expresses. A day here would bring untold delights and the shed was host to many famous engines. An old favourite of the Great Central in the late 1950s was 'A3' No. 60102 *Sir Frederick Banbury* looking solid and ready for anything in the autumn sunshine of 29th October 1961. She died a month later! 35;2

Plate 71: **34F GRANTHAM** When the German Federal smoke deflectors were added to some 'A3's, there was endless controversy. They seemed strange to begin with, but, in retrospect, they certainly did nothing to harm their looks. No. 60112 *St. Simon* amply proves the point, just ex-Doncaster Works, in the sun of 20th October 1962.   2

Plate 72: **36A DONCASTER** Early-morning shed visits had an atmosphere all their own. Often the mists still lay about and there was an air of things being readied for the day. The two men (right) seem uncertain with their diesel, whereas driver and fireman of 'Mogul' No. 43146, know precisely what to do, even if they can hardly see their charge – she was in her last month of running. 3rd January 1965. 182;*3*

Plate 73: **36A DONCASTER** The charm of Doncaster was the variety, the ex-works engines, but also the unusual. Here, some strange accident seems to have befallen '04/1' 2-8-0 No. 63618 – she is minus buffers! 25th March 1962. *2*

Plate 74: **36C FRODINGHAM**
Occasionally, shed sites gave superb
chances of locomotive studies. A case in
point, at Frodingham, is '02/3' 2-8-0 No.
63973, standing as if proud of having her
photograph taken! 27th May 1962. 70;*1*

Plate 75: **36E RETFORD** Although only
one code, Retford was, in fact, two distinct
shed sites, separated by the main line and
more than just distance. The appearance
and character of the two were totally
different. In the Great Northern yard,
'J11/3' 0-6-0 No. 64354 quietly awaits
the next call. 27th May 1962.   64;*1*

Plate 76: **36E RETFORD** The scene is the GC shed this time, on Sunday 14th June 1964. '04/8' No. 63726 shows signs of hard work, with a bent running plate, standing under the typical GC leg-crane, whilst 'Austerity' No. 90577 seems the only engine ready to move; sister '04/8' No. 63914 and 'B1' No. 61213 are stored, withdrawn. *1*

Plate 77: **40A LINCOLN** 'B1's in conversation? Nos. 61069 and 61026 *Ourebi* are seen from the coaches of 'The Mallard Commemorative Rail Tour', on Saturday, 6th July 1963. Hauled by 'A4' No. 60007 *Sir Nigel Gresley*, the train went outwards from Kings Cross to Doncaster, via Lincoln.   64:2

Plate 78: **40B IMMINGHAM** With the docks nearby, Immingham had to handle many heavy freight trains. Some, like the famed fish trains, required fast running, but others could take a more leisurely pace, which is where '04/7' No. 63615 would come in. Her front end is remarkably clean. 22nd April 1961.   120;2

Plate 79: **40B IMMINGHAM** Some of the variety of motive power used by the shed, can be seen in this view, taken from inside the shed building. Left to right: '04/8' No. 63607, unidentified 'B1', 'Mogul' No. 43142 and 'K3' No. 61956. 22nd April 1961.   2

Plates 80 & 81: **40E COLWICK** On the last day of the Great Central out of Marylebone — 3rd September 1966 — several specials were run. Perhaps the rarest motive power was 'Merchant Navy' No. 35030 *Elder Dempster Lines* which worked through to Nottingham. **Above,** she is seen at Colwick, with 'Jubilee' No. 45562 *Alberta* in the background. **Below:** A closer view of *Alberta* on the shed's turntable. Once the fourth biggest allocation, Colwick closed to steam three months later.   Both 199;*3*

Plate 82: **41A SHEFFIELD (DARNALL)** In view of diesel's infiltration, in the early 1960s, things look bad here for '04/3' ex-ROD 2-8-0 No. 63846, in the hands of No. D4034, but she actually survived a further two years. 28th October 1962.   95;1L

Plate 83: **41A SHEFFIELD (DARNALL)**
Looking very much the worse for wear,
'B1' No. 61211 is dumped in the shed
yard, awaiting further attention. 28th
October 1962.   *1L*

Plate 84: **41D CANKLOW** Although in the ER codes, Canklow was an ex-Midland shed, with, in 1950, an exclusively Midland allocation. The position still looks the same, on 14th June 1964, as 'Jubilee' No. 45620 *North Borneo* simmers quietly, without name-plates.   54;*1*

Plate 85: **41E STAVELEY (BARROW HILL)** The delight of a visit to Barrow Hill, was the sight of the small engines, used in the nearby Steel Works. On 14th June 1964, Johnson 1F 0-6-0T No. 41734 stands in the shed yard, between duties. Over 80 years old when photographed, she lasted until December 1966 – close to the end of steam.   71;*1*

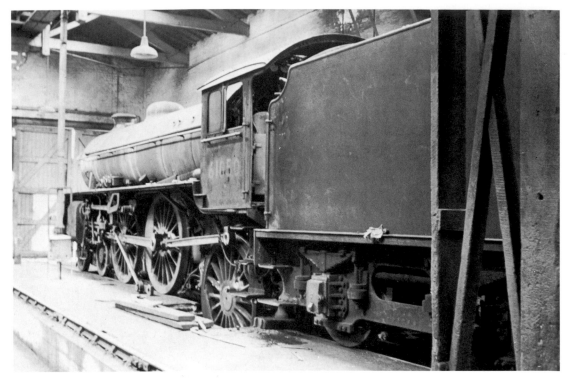

Plate 86: **41F MEXBOROUGH** Another heavy freight shed, it was host to the only ER Garrett – No. 69999 – for 25 years, to help on the Worsborough Bank. Long connected with the Woodhead route to Manchester, from Sheffield, it had a massive allocation in the 1950s. Electrification took its toll, however, and when 'B1' No. 61050 was photographed, on 14th June 1964, she was the only engine on shed!   120;*1*

Plate 87: **41J LANGWITH JUNCTION** Another shed that had a healthy allocation in steam days, it saw its work gradually disappear in the early 1960s. '04/8' No. 63691 and '04/3' NO. 63679 (ex-ROD) appear to be comparing their fates, on 14th June 1964. Both lasted another 11 months.   61;*1*

Plate 88: **50A YORK (SOUTH)** Like Blackpool, York had North and South sheds. The latter was the less fashionable, but still housed interesting locos. Station pilot, 'J72' No. 68736, has a rest, on shed, for a while, on 23rd April 1961. Nothing now remains of this site. 176(between the two sheds);2

Plate 89: **50A YORK (NORTH)** ER 'Λ2's were a small class, but the variety therein was great. One of the originals of the class, now 'A2/2', No. 60502 *Earl Marischal* carries the rather weird chimney smoke deflectors. 'B1' No. 61039 *Steinbok* is companion. 23rd April 1961.   2

Plate 90: **50A YORK (NORTH)** The home of 'Q6' 0-8-0 No. 63344 – once one of the shed's roundhouses, now home for the National Railway Museum.   *3*

Plate 91: **50B HULL (DAIRYCOATES)** This shed at Hull, was a strange mixture of buildings and 'missing' buildings, with an open-air roundhouse. Seen here, in the sunshine of 12th May 1962, are: 'Austerity' No. 90623, 'Mogul' No. 43078 and 'B1' No. 61010 *Wildebeeste.* Note the shed's habit of marking buffers 'XX'!   *144;2*

Plate 92: **50B HULL (DAIRYCOATES)**
The 'K3' 2-6-0 was an honest workhorse –
often unsung, but reliable. No. 61847
looks every inch the part in the shed yard,
on 22nd April 1961.   *2*

Plate 93: **53C HULL (SPRINGHEAD)** One
of four sheds in the city, Springhead closed
early and, therefore, was not seen by most
enthusiasts. The actual shed buildings have
disappeared, leaving the 'B16s' out in the
open. Nos. 61436 and 61425 head their
respective rows, on 22nd April 1961.
54;2 (including Alexandra Dock)

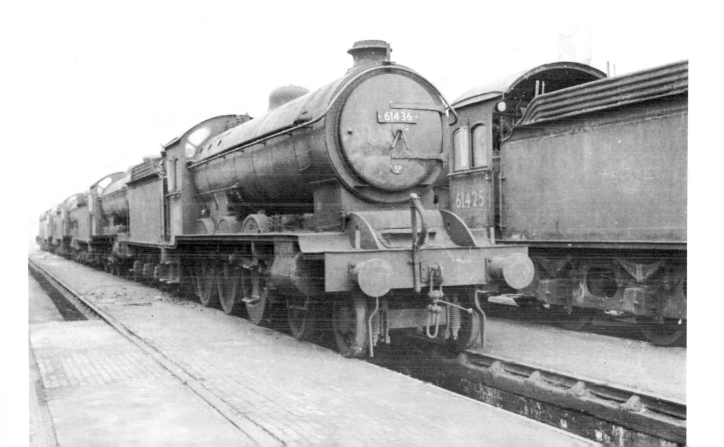

Plate 94: **50D GOOLE** It was a long trek to Goole shed and, on Sunday 30th March 1963, it was frustrating to get no closer than this shot. The reason was that No. D6733 (centre) had been set afire the day before, by persons unknown and was still smouldering! The foreman, somewhat understandably, was rather irate! Also seen are 'Austerity' No. 90186, Nos. D2598, 90704 and 'Mogul' No. 43125.   34;*1L*

Plate 95: **50F MALTON** Malton's allocation was small, enough only to cope with local duties and a couple for Pickering sub-shed. It would seem, from the condition of 'J27' No. 65849, that the shed staff kept their engines reasonably clean – indeed, the whole scene exudes a well kept air. 23rd April 1961.   16;*2*

Plate 56: **51A DARLINGTON** Like other sheds with Works close by, Darlington saw ex-works engines. 'A3' No. 60036 *Colombo* certainly looks in this state, in the southern end of the shed yard, on 29th August 1964. The wind was cold, but the late evening sun gives a special edge to the colour – she was withdrawn three months later. 117:1

Plate 97: **51A DARLINGTON** As *Colombo*, above, was stand-by for failed engines, so 'V2' 2-6-2 No. 60806 was stand-by for the 'A3'! Seen in company with local freight engines, the view is earlier in the day than above.   3

Plate 98: **51A DARLINGTON** Apart from the engine number, the picture is timeless. This railman seems concerned with other than his charge, 'Q6' 0-8-0 No. 63357, which simmers quietly in the background. 23rd April 1961.   *2*

Plate 99: **51C WEST HARTLEPOOL** When the sun shone, holes in the roof made attractive patterns in the shed. The building is totally inhabited by 'Austeritys', No. 90434 is nearest the camera, with Nos. 90135, 90210, 90116 and 90459 in front. Just seen through the left portal, No. 90254 leans at a dangerous angle, having jumped the tracks! 1st July 1967.   *77;1*

Plate 100: **51C WEST HARTLEPOOL** An unhappy end for 'Q6' No. 63397 epitomizes the state that many steam engines reached in the last decade of steam on BR. The engine has only just been withdrawn, but, already, the front number-plate has gone. 1st July 1967. *1*

Plate 101: 51F WEST AUCKLAND
Freight was the *raison d'être* of West
Auckland shed. In 1950 there was much
variety in the allocation but, strangely, no
'Q6's. The position had changed by 1st
July 1962, however, as can be seen by the
shed-plate on No. 63446.   40;2

Plate 102: 51J NORTHALLERTON
Northallerton never had a big allocation and
the emphasis was on local passenger, with
the occasional freight. Standard Class 2
2-6-0 No. 78011 is ideally suited for both,
as she waits between duties, on 23rd April
1961. When the shed closed, not long
after, No. 78011 was transferred to the
MR, to end her days at Trafford Park.
13;2

Overleaf: *Plate 103: 52A GATESHEAD* Immediately south of the river at Newcastle, Gateshead
was a very difficult shed to bunk, the foreman being very strict. But any visit did pay dividends, as
a second glimpse of 'J72' No. 68736 shows *(see plate 88)*, this time seen in full glorious colour
and over a year later, on 1st July 1962. Although still bearing a 50A shed-plate, she had just
been transferred to Gateshead.   89;2

*Plate 104: **52A GATESHEAD** The corrugated iron and wooden structure betrays an early history for these shed buildings, but they don't look out of place beside a none-too-spotless 'V2' No. 60939. 29th August 1964.   3*

Plate 105: **52B HEATON** This was a strange shed. Not huge buildings, but an allocation bigger than Gateshead and of a bewildering variety. It was not unknown for 'A4's to hob-knob with out-and-out freight engines, with no apparent good reason; and large and small were common, as can be seen by 'J72' No. 69008 in company with an 'A1'. 15th June 1962.   119;*2*

Plate 106: **52C BLAYDON** The first half of February 1963 was particularly bad for snow; the photographer travelled through 8ft. drifts, from Leicester, in a minibus, to 'do' the Newcastle sheds! Blaydon can be seen after the blizzard, housing stored locos: 'J39' No. 64852, 'V3' Nos. 67657 and 67687, 'A2/3' No. 60521 *Watling Street*, 'J39' No. 64864 and 'V2' No. 60934, among others, on Sunday 17th. 79;*1L*

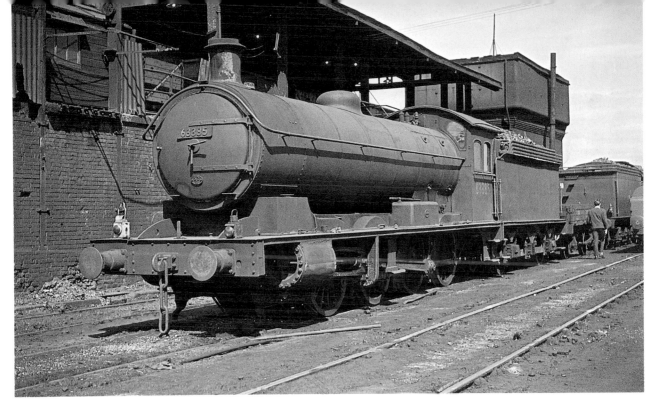

Plate 107: **52C BLAYDON** In balmier days, seven months earlier, 'Q6' No. 63385 stands over the ash pits, whilst remnants of a spotters' group move towards an interesting looking tender. 1st July 1962. *2*

Plate 108: **52D TWEEDMOUTH** 23rd April 1962 and looking at 'J39/1' No. 64868 and 'J39/2' No. 64925 they appear to be in fine condition and ready for more work. Unfortunately, they are both in store – No. 64868 already withdrawn and No. 64925 formally eight months later. Both spent all their BR days at Tweedmouth, with the former being shipped out to Alnmouth sub. *47;2 (14 at Alnmouth)*

Plate 109: **52D SUB-ALNMOUTH** The sub actually outlasted the parent shed, Alnmouth being closed almost exactly 12 months after Tweedmouth. Less than two years to closure, 'K1' 2-6-0 No. 62011 stands with guard's van in the evening sunshine of 28th August 1964. Note the glint of the sun on the wheel flanges. 14;*1L*

Plate 110: **52F NORTH BLYTH** In that same evening sun, of 28th August 1964, 'Q6' No. 63413 makes a fine silhouette on the ramp, in the shed yard. Over the water from South Blyth, North shed was by far the more interesting.   44;*1* (including 18 at South)

Plate 111: **52F NORTH BLYTH** This time we are inside the shed roundhouse and a Midland influence is apparent. Prototype 'Mogul' No. 43000 stands in company with sister engine No. 43055. Interestingly, neither have a shed-plate, probably because the latter has just been withdrawn and No. 43000 follows a month later. 1st July 1967.   *1*

Plate 112: **52G SUNDERLAND** Sunderland's roundhouses were quite bright, making for good photographs. 'J27' 0-6-0 No. 65872 makes a pleasing sight in 1963, as she stands quietly beneath a dangerous light bulb in a shed that she knew the whole of her BR days.   58;*3*

Plate 113: **52G SUNDERLAND** The bright sunshine and clear lining of 'B1' No. 61035 *Pronghorn* make for another pleasing picture at this shed, this time outside the straight shed, in 1964.   *3*

Plate 114: **52H TYNE DOCK** Heavy freight was the bread and butter of Tyne Dock shed and, after they were introduced, the specially modified Standard '9Fs' did truly sterling service. Here No. 92063 takes a welcome breather, on 29th August 1964.   *3*

Plate 1.5: **52H TYNE DOCK** Sheds could be photographically infuriating, but they also presented great opportunities. The pylon reflection, on the gap in the wall, focuses the eye on the brickwork and the tantalizing glimpse of an 'Q6', to make a truly artistic railway photograph. 29th August 1954   48/L

Plate 116: **52K CONSETT** A typical railway picture, with paraphernalia strewn everywhere and engines seemingly parking where they can. Not a big shed, with a small allocation, it was often host to visitors. Here, 'Q6' Nos. 63354 and 63439 (the latter at Consett all its BR life), wait for the next call from the Steel Works. 1st July 1962.   10:2

Plate 117: **53D BRIDLINGTON** Dead during the week, Bridlington shed came alive at summer weekends, as the holiday specials poured in. Taking all the available parking spaces, bathing in a hot summer's sun, the engines await their return trains, with 'B1' No. 61303 apparently uncertain which special she is due to haul! 7th August 1961.   10:2

Plate 118: **55A LEEDS (HOLBECK)** A bright sun shines outside the roundhouse and picks out parts of 'Jubilee' No. 45593 *Kolhapur*. Although she has another 18 months of life left with BR (before preservation), she has already lost her nameplate. 24th April 1966.　96;3

Plate 119: **55A LEEDS (HOLBECK)** In another roundhouse, less glamorous parts of Holbeck's stud take pause. Left to right, in front of the quasi-cathedral windows, are: 'Mogul' No. 43076, '8F' No. 48158 (with snowplough), 'Black 5' No. 44943 (with a graceful plume of steam) and No. 45219 (with smokebox door open). 1st July 1967.　*1*

Plate 120: **55B STOURTON** 'Clan Pacifics' were rare visitors south of Carlisle and even more so on freight sheds. The working is unknown but, out of place in Stourton yard, No. 72006 *Clan Mackenzie* has less than a month to get back home. Withdrawn in May 1966, she is seen here on 24th April.   48;*3*

Plate 121: **55C FARNLEY JUNCTION** A mixture of express passenger and heavy freight, its allocation added to the pleasure of visiting this shed, which often had engines conveniently parked in the open. Here, 'Jubilee' No. 45647 *Sturdee* seems not to mind the rain, in the spring of 1965.   50;*3*

Plate 122: **55D ROYSTON** '8F' No. 48113 has obviously been working in dusty conditions, but this merely picks out the motion details and enhances the look of the engine. Serving Royston for the whole of her BR life, No. 48113 was withdrawn 18 months after this picture. May 1966.   61;*3*

Plate 123: **55D ROYSTON** Another view of No. 48113, this time sharing the limelight with sister engine No. 48093, another engine that didn't stray from Royston in BR days. The two were withdrawn at the same time.   *3*

Plate 124: **55E NORMANTON** MR '4F' 0-6-0 No. 44400's tender is stacked high, presumably in anticipation of hard work. Bearing the cab-side diagonal streak, a warning for West Coast main line electric cables, she looks an ideal subject for any modeller. April 1965.   48;*3*

Plate 125: **55F BRADFORD MAN-NINGHAM** In later years, Manningham made use of many Fairburn 2-6-4Ts, often for hauling the Bradford portions of expresses to Leeds. Here, No. 42252 is quiet between duties, in May 1966. 45;*3*

Plate 126: **55H LEEDS (NEVILLE HILL)**
Initially the second shed to York and handling the bulk of the ER workings around
Leeds, Neville Hill had both a healthy and
varied allocation. The variety was aided
early in 1966, by the housing of preserved
'K4' No. 3442 *The Great Marquess.* 81;3

Plate 127: **55H LEEDS (NEVILLE HILL)**
Six months earlier than the previous
photograph and 'A1' No. 60154 *Bon
Accord* ekes out the last few weeks of her
life, as stand-by for engine failures. Here,
she simmers quietly in the late-summer
sun of 1965.   *3*

Plate 128: **55H LEEDS (NEVILLE HILL)**
The shed's yard was a nice open place,
ideal for photographs. Going further back
in time from the previous two views, 'B16/
1' No. 61415 shows off the typical Raven
design, on 23rd April 1961.   *2*

Plate 129: **56A WAKEFIELD** The view on
entrance to the shed, on 3rd March 1963,
looks rather as if some spoilt child has left
his toys scattered about! It would be
interesting to know where the parts
belonged, but presumably not to 'B1' No.
61019 *Nilghai* by the look of her!   123;*1*

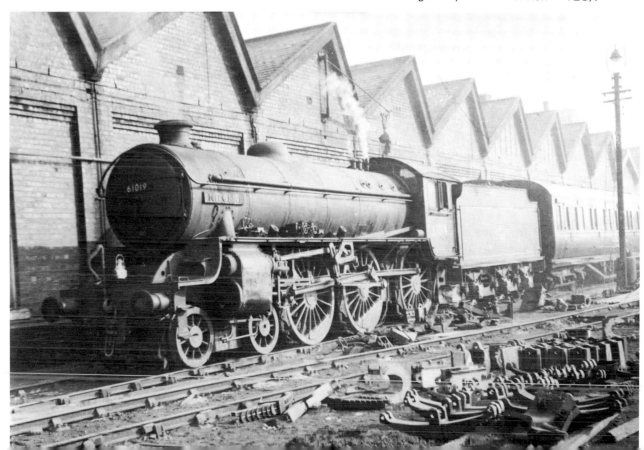

Plate 130: **56A WAKEFIELD** The spring sunshine of 24th April 1966 picks out the details of what is a typical-looking 'Austerity', in normal BR steam days. They always seemed to have oil running freely and No. 90382 is no exception. *3*

Plate 131: **56B ARDSLEY** '04/8' No. 63864 and her companions are nearly dwarfed by the shed's coal stocks, but they will not want any of it themselves, as they are all stored. 21st July 1962. 88:2

Plate 132: **56B ARDSLEY** 'V2' No. 60843 looks in good condition but, seen here in September 1965, she has only a month to live. This was a typical scene, in straight sheds and one taken so much for granted at the time.   *3*

Plate 133: **56C COPLEY HILL** Copley's allocation in the early 1950s was predominantly freight, but with a handful of 'A3's and 'A1's for variety. Less than two and a half years before the shed closed completely, 'A3's No. 60039 *Sandwich* and No. 60082 *Neil Gow* look glad to get out of the rain. 19th May 1962.   *39;2*

Plate 134: **56C COPLEY HILL** The wet conditions are self evident and the rain is attempting a slight clean on 'J6' 0-6-0 No. 64226's boiler! To the left of the engine is the foreman's office. 20th May 1962.   2

Plate 135: **56E SOWERBY BRIDGE** The day is dull and damp, but Aspinall's '3F' 0-6-0 No. 52121 still looks fine, on Sunday 21st October 1962. She has, however, a 'Not To Be Moved' notice on her and she succumbed to progress two months later.   33;2

Plate 136: **60A INVERNESS** Pickersgill's '3P' 4-4-0's did sterling work throughout Scotland for the Caledonian and, later, the LMS, but, here, NO. 54466 somewhat shyly peeps out of Inverness shed. Seen on 3rd June 1962, she still looks in good condition, despite having been withdrawn in March! 58;2

Plates 137 & 138: **60B AVIEMORE** The time is 21st April 1962 and diesels are beginning to find their way to the remoter parts. Aviemore is feeling the wind of change and looks deserted at first glance **(above)**. Engines are there, however, although most are in store. MR '4F' No. 44258 **(below)** is a case in point, though not yet actually withdrawn.   7;2

Plate 139: **61A KITTYBREWSTER** The scaffolding betrays the fact that a new roundhouse is being built, which, judging by the clouds, is well needed. Open to the elements on 12th August 1956 are: 'J36' No. 65228, Standard 4 2-6-4Ts Nos. 80021 and 80028, 'Z5' No. 68192, 'B1' No. 61400, 'J36' No. 65222 and Class 4 No. 80108.   70;2

Plate 140: **61B FERRYHILL** Ash disposal seems to be a problem, on 26th August 1964, as 'A4' No. 60034 *Lord Faringdon* awaits her turn to be cleaned out. Externally, she could do with attention as well, as she is hardly recognizable as being in green livery, under all the dirt!   40;1

Plate 141: **61B FERRYHILL** In contrast to *Lord Faringdon,* 'A2' No. 60527 *Sun Chariot* is resplendent in her green coat. 7th June 1962.   2

Plate 142: **62A THORNTON** Still in the stock lists and working, 'N15' 0-6-2T No. 69204 has obviously not seen the inside of works for some time. Bearing the old Lion & Wheel symbol, but no shed-plate, she stands among the shed debris, on 22nd April 1962, just five months before the end.   112;2

Plate 143: **62A THORNTON** 'J38' 0-6-0 No. 65925 looks well enough, but her perch, by the pit, looks rather precarious! The picture well illustrates the scene that was the epitome of steam sheds. 27th August 1964. *1*

Plate 144: **62B DUNDEE (TAY BRIDGE)** A scene common in steam days was the engine on a turntable. Facing one way may have had its drawbacks, but the tables gave for photographic variety. 'B1' No. 61262 awaits her driver's attention, on 27th August 1964.   101;*1*

Plate 145: **62B DUNDEE (TAY BRIDGE)** Such was the highland weather, that tender extensions were added, to try and give the locomen more protection; how successful these were, is uncertain. One of the last of this class to remain in service, 'J36' No. 65319 rests, temporarily out of use, on 22nd April 1962.   *2*

Plate 146: **62B SUB-MONTROSE** Not so much a sub-shed, more a stabling point, the photographer finds 'J37' 0-6-0 No. 64597 simmering quietly, while her crew take advantage of the hut's amenities. 27th August 1964.   *1*

Plate 147: **62C SUB-ALLOA** On 22nd April 1962, Alloa shed is chock-a-block. Only a 2-road shed, there is only room in the yard for 'J38' (rebuilt with 'J39' boiler) No. 65906, standing in front of the strange corrugated contraption.   *2*

Plate 148: **62C DUNFERMLINE** Anticipating the Health & Safety At Work Act, Dunfermline has clearly painted the point levers and they stand out well, in front of Standard 4 2-6-0 No. 76110, on 22nd April 1962. 75;2

Plate 149: **62C DUNFERMLINE** The late afternoon sun is beginning to sink, as 'J6' No. 65288 gently pollutes the clear summer air. Surviving at Dunfermline until June 1967, No. 65288 fought off the challenge of the diesel, seen right. 27th August 1964. *1*

Plate 150: **63A PERTH** The following plates are three views of variety at Perth. 'Clan' 4-6-2 No. 72005 *Clan Macgregor* collects coal from the plant, on 5th June 1962, while the sign seems to point to Australia, rather than Greenock! 2

Plate 151: Sticking out like a sore thumb, Highland Railway No. 103 is in marked contrast to her surroundings. Behind, also preserved, is 'D34' No. 256 *Glen Douglas,* while to the left, is 'Britannia' No. 70019 *Lightning* and 'V2' No. 60980. 8th June 1962. 2

Plate 152: The evening is drawing in and gives a dramatic edge to 'Royal Scot' No. 46166 *London Rifle Brigade* and her oil lamp. One of the last batch to be withdrawn, her trip from here back to Carlisle, was probably her last; seen on 25th August 1964, she was withdrawn a fortnight later.   138;1

Plate 153: **63A SUB-FORFAR** Once a shed in its own right – as 63C – Forfar had been relegated to a store for dumped engines by the time this photograph was taken on 9th July 1962. Just over 20 years on and it has no railway at all! When seen, ex-Caledonian '2P' 0-4-4T No. 55204, was one of the last three of the class working; she was withdrawn in January 1963 and dumped at the back of Perth shed.   21;1

Plate 154: **63A SUB-FORFAR** Seen from a different vantage point, a month earlier, the row of stored engines can be glimpsed to the left of the shed. In the foreground, 'Black 5' No. 45472 heads north on a freight. The extent of the railway presence now ended, can easily be seen. 7th June 1962.   2

Plates 155 & 156: **63B FORT WILLIAM** Two views of the shed and 'Black 5' No. 44975, on 20th April 1962. **Above:** Snow can be seen on Ben Nevis and, although the sun shines brightly, the clouds look ominous, as No. 44975 stands at the back of the shed. 12;2. **Below:** An interesting comparison in snowploughs can be seen, on No. 44975 and '4F' No. 44255. The latter also has a special tender, for extra protection. *2*

Plate 157: **63B SUB-MALLAIG** The view of the shed from the sea edge shows 'K2/2' No. 61789 *Loch Laidon* in fine fettle, on 14th August 1957. Although summer, it is raining, but this is still 'heaven' compared to some of the weathers endured by the shed.　　*2*

Plate 158: **64A ST. MARGARETS** A strange shed to visit, entered through a passageway and split by the main line (!), it had its fair share of interesting locos and the second biggest allocation of all. One such loco, was 'Y9' 0-4-0ST No. 68095 and, as seen on 13th July 1962, she is parked beside St. Margarets unique brickwork. She was withdrawn six months later.　　*220;1*

Plate 159: **64A ST. MARGARETS** The
work on the shed roof looks interesting,
but somewhat perilous, behind last-
numbered 'N15' 0-6-2T No. 69224. Note
also, the works plate on the sandbox, con-
firming her number. 23rd April 1962.   2

Plate 160: **64B HAYMARKET** The tran-
sition from steam to diesel is obviously
under way. No. D5311 (left) and No.
D366 (right) stake their claim, but 'A3' No.
60078 *Night Hawk* fights on. Here
shedded at Gateshead, she was briefly
transferred to Heaton and then withdrawn
seven months after this photograph was
taken. 23rd April 1962.   79;2

Plate 161: **64B HAYMARKET** Yet another Gateshead engine, visiting Edinburgh, this time 'A4' No. 60002 *Sir Murrough Wilson.* Seen on 13th July 1962, her size looks truly impressive next to 'J36' No. 65288. *1*

Plate 162: **64C DALRY ROAD** Withdrawn from ordinary service in July 1961, the last of the class, 'D49/1' No. 62712 *Morayshire,* with GC tender, was temporarily stored at Dalry Road, until restored to her former glory, as LNER No. 246. 13th July 1962. *46;1*

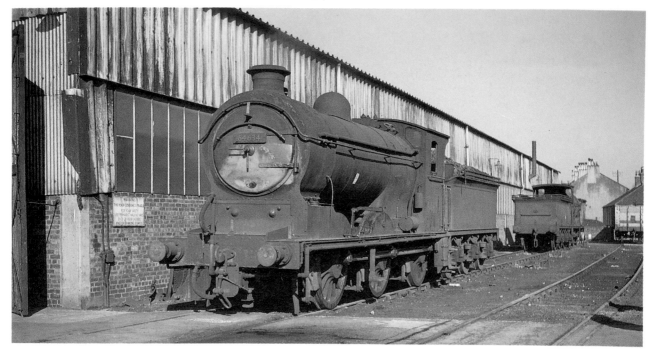

Plate 163: **64F BATHGATE** Judging by the badly burnt smokebox, 'J37' 0-6-0 No. 64634 has been worked very hard in the not-too-distant past! The clear Scottish sunshine shows her condition well and also shows up the ATC equipment. 23rd April 1962.   38;2

Plate 164: **64F BATHGATE** The shed buildings were next to the main line and this view of Standard 4 2-6-0 No. 76106 is taken from an Edinburgh train. With the smoke behind, she is silhouetted well, as is the driver reaching for his locker. 24th August 1964.   *3*

Plate 165: **64G HAWICK** Like Bathgate, Hawick was situated beside the main line. Standard 2 2-6-0 No. 78047 looks creditably clean, at the side of the shed, on 9th July 1961, on a site that is now a sports centre! In 1950, the shed was home to two dozen ER engines.   24;2

Plate 166. **65A EASTFIELD** The date is 5th June 1956 and diesel shunters have arrived. The shed's 'J50' 0-6-0Ts have been displaced, but only temporarily, as 'J50/3' No. 68957, at least, hung on until 1960.   164;2

Plate 167: **65B ST. ROLLOX** With
evidence of a large development under way
in the background, 'Black 5' No. 45374
blows off excess steam, in St. Rollox yard.
Actually shedded at Aston, she has presumably just been through the Works
nearby. 25th August 1964.   77;1

Plate 168: **65B ST. ROLLOX** We are at
the side of the main line now and 'Jubilee'
No. 45742 *Connaught* is having her ash
raked out. 25th August 1964.   3

Plate 169: **65C PARKHEAD** 'J37' 0-6-0 No. 64609, standing proudly in the yard, is set off by the unusual roof-line and the magnificent signal box, seen to the left. At Parkhead for the whole of her BR life, No. 64609 has obviously been well cared for, but not to lasting effect, as she was withdrawn seven months later. 10th June 1962.   68;*2*

Plate 170: **65D DAWSHOLM** Very shortly after taking this photograph, the photographer backed his car into a buffer stop in the shed yard (!), but that did not detract from the delight of seeing bright green ex-Caledonian 4-2-2 No. 123. Note the thistle on the buffer! 10th July 1962. 43;*1*

Plate 171: **65E KIPPS** Although an allocation in excess of 50 in the early 1950s, Kipps cannot have had many stranger-looking engines than 'J36' No. 65285. The standard chimney can be seen behind, but No. 65285 has been 'doctored', to serve on branch lines around Glasgow. 22nd April 1962.   53;2

Plate 172: **65F GRANGEMOUTH** In the early 1950s the shed's allocation was exclusively Midland and 'Austerity', but, by 23rd April 1962, things had changed. 'J36' No. 65257 looks smart and full of promises, with her very full tender, in direct competition with the diesel's stripes!   36;2

Plate 179: **65J STIRLING** Looking north, Stirling's small shed had a quasi-cathedral portal and this superbly frames 'Black 5' No. 45475, on 25th August 1964.   49/3

Plate 174: **65J STIRLING** A more distant view of the shed, shows a healthy occupation, on Friday 8th June 1962. Nearest to the camera are, left to right: 'Black 5's Nos. 45213 (partially in the shed) and 45359 and Standard 4 2-6-4T No. 80062.   2

Plate 175: **65K POLMONT** Around 'J38' No. 65909, standing proudly in the sun, the buildings are typical early sheds – wooden offices, shed doors and parts of the roof missing. Seen on 23rd April 1962, the depot was finally closed in May 1964.   43;2

Plate 176: **66B MOTHERWELL** 'Black 5'
No. 44908 is showing signs of hard work
around the boiler end and appears to be in
need of the rest, on 24th August 1964.
115;*3*

Plate 177: **66D GREENOCK (LADY-
BURN)** A lot of space and not much to fill
it! The shed roof obviously leaks and,
therefore, the railman in the pit is not
going to have a very pleasant job! Fairburn
2-6-4T No. 42216 looks on, whilst one of
the other seven engines on shed, can be
seen in the background. 24th August
1964.   42;*1*

Plate 178: **67A CORKERHILL** The evening sun really brings out the best photogenically from Standard 2-6-4T No. 80063 and it looks as though someone has been busy with an oily rag on the smokebox, as the rest of the engine is filthy. 24th August 1964.   91;7

Plate 179: 67B HURLFORD The grass in the foreground looks to have a struggle to take hold, but the clouds above may help soon. Meanwhile, Standard 3 2-6-0 No. 77015 simmers quietly, on 11th June 1962. 56:2

Plate 180: **67C AYR** More cathedral styling can be seen behind 'Crabs' Nos. 42737 and 42803, on 23rd August 1964. 59;1. Plate 181: As can be seen, this class held sway on this day. No. 42737 can again be seen, nearest to the camera, whilst No. 42801 is in mid-distance. *3*

Plates 182 & 183: **67E DUMFRIES** Two views of the shed yard showing totally contrasting natures, but separated by only two years! **Above:** 'J72' No. 68750 is seen out of use, on 6th August 1962. Although transferred to Dumfries, she was never used there and finally 'died' in December 1962. 38;2. **Below:** Looking more like the Midland shed it was originally, 'Black 5' No. 45053 holds sway in the yard, in the rain of 22nd August 1964. *1*

Plate 184: 70A **NINE ELMS** Sadly, none of this scene is now recognizable, the re-sited Covent Garden fruit and vegetable market currently in its place. In happier days, 'Merchant Navy' No. 35013 *Blue Funnel* looks immaculate in the shed yard. 19th July 1964.   *100:1*

Plate 185: **70A NINE ELMS** A different and less usual view this time, showing 'S15' 4-6-0 astride the ash pit. A not untypical scene of steam sheds. 21st January 1962.   *2*

Plate 186: **70B FELTHAM** Photographically, Feltham was an excellent shed to visit as many of the engines would be out in the open. On 19th July 1964, another 'S15' No. 30837, is a case in point. This engine was another to have spent all her BR days at one shed.   *77;1*

Plate 187: **70C GUILDFORD** Guildford was a cramped shed; seemingly pushed into chalk cliffs, it had only a small straight shed and, a rarity, half a roundhouse! 'USA' tank No. 30064 can be seen against one wall of the latter, on 19th July 1964. Judging by her condition, she was treated with loving care.   57;*1*

Plate 188: **70D BASINGSTOKE** Face to face, Standard 5 4-6-0 No. 73029 could almost be showing off to 'poorer' cousin, 'Class 4' 2-6-0 No. 76031, who looks very drab in comparison with the very attractive green. The scene is 2nd July 1967, just a couple of weeks from the end of steam on the Southern, at which time both these locos were withdrawn.   22;*1*

Plate 189: **70E* READING SOUTH** Never a big shed, the sight of Southern engines so far into the GW heartland, was reward enough. With the GW main line in the background, yet another 'S15', this time No. 30496, stands on shed, having worked an unidentified special, in the summer of 1962.   18;*3*

Plate 190: **70E SALISBURY** Salisbury never had a huge allocation, but there always seemed to be a lot on shed. In the depth of the building, SR diesel No. 15232 can just be seen, extreme left, whilst Ivatt 2-6-2T No. 41300 pokes her nose into the light. To the right, stand 'Merchant Navy' No. 35006 *Peninsular & Oriental S. N. Co* and Standard 4 No. 76018. 21st June 1964.   57;*1*

Plate 191: **7OE SALISBURY** Looking immaculate in the early summer sun of May 1965, 'Merchant Navy' No. 35017 *Belgian Marine* quietly awaits the arrival of an enthusiasts' special, which she is due to work to Exeter. 3

Plate 192: **7OH RYDE** Right up to the end of steam, visiting the Isle of Wight Railway was like stepping back in time. Quaint little engines travelled picturesque lines to dainty stations. Of the two sheds on the island, Ryde was the smaller, but lasted the longer. Here, No. W21 *Sandown* stands in the company of No. W30 *Shorwell*. 2nd May 1965.   12:3

Plate 193: **71A EASTLEIGH** With the Works and the shed's large allocation, Eastleigh was the Southern's premier depot. The engines were very varied and express locos abounded. Here, 'Battle of Britain Pacific' No. 34076 *41 Squadron,* still unrebuilt, stands under the starter signal, long a feature of Eastleigh. 21st June 1964.   145;1

Plate 194: **71A EASTLEIGH** During a visit, one was bound to see withdrawn engines, awaiting disposal. 'A1X' 0-6-0T has been withdrawn seven months here, but still looks highly presentable. Behind is 'B4' No. 30102. 21st June 1964.   1

Plate 195: **71B BOURNEMOUTH** Easily
seen from the station, this was a good
shed for spotters. On a summer's day in
1965, there is plenty of steam about, as
Ivatt sisters Nos. 41284 and 41312 face
the sun, awaiting their next turn. Both were
later transferred to Nine Elms and
withdrawn in mid-1967.   52;3

Plate 196: **71D FRATTON** The shed for
Portsmouth, the building and the allocation
suffered in later years and 'L1' No. 31757,
here, looks particularly lonely. Seen on
Sunday, 8th July 1962, she had been con-
demned eight months earlier.   49;2

Plate 197: **71G WEYMOUTH** Out on a limb from the mainstream of SR activity, the shed, nevertheless, lasted until the end of SR steam in 1967. Originally a GWR shed, with exclusively WR engines, the balance shifted in the late 1950s/early 1960s. Here, Rebuilt 'Battle of Britain' No. 34087 *145 Squadron* seeks attention, on a day when the shed was visited by 'A4' *Sir Nigel Gresley*!   32;*3*

Plate 198: **72A EXMOUTH JUNCTION** A classic, three-quarter view of unrebuilt 'Battle of Britain' No. 34064 *Fighter Command* simmering quietly on shed, with No. 34108 *Wincanton* behind, on 21st August 1961.   122;*1*

Plates 199 & 200: **Parent and sub-shed. (Above): 72A EXMOUTH JUNCTION** A superb view of the shed front, with 18 locos visible and demonstrating some of the variety to be found. 16th September 1962. *2.* **(Below): 72A SUB-OKEHAMPTON** Set high on the hills above the town, the shed was a windy place, but here, though, things look calmer. Class U No. 31636 stands at the approach to the turntable, on 15th September 1962. *2*

Plate 201: 72E BARNSTAPLE JUNCTION The view at 6.50 a.m. (!), on 29th August 1964. A Southern shed, but housing MR and WR locos. Ivatt No. 41208 has come up from Exeter and '4300' Class 2-6-0 No. 5336 has worked in on the long-since lifted Taunton-Barnstaple line.   13:2

Plate 202: **72F WADEBRIDGE** Wadebridge was famous for the Adams tanks, but there is no sign of them here, as the shed is temporary home to GW tanks Nos. 4694 and 1369 and SR 'Battle of Britain' No. 34078 *222 Squadron.* 16th September 1962.   5;2

Plate 203: **73A STEWARTS LANE** Split into two, the foreman was very touchy at letting spotters into the electric half! Entrance to the steam part was relatively easy and, on 29th April 1962, Class C No. 31588 sports a healthy supply of coal. A few weeks after this, she was transferred to Ashford and withdrawn in July.   112;1

Plate 204: **75B REDHILL** The shed was actually closed 11 months after this photograph, but matters do not look too bright here, on 19th July 1964. Class N No. 31873 is cold and without shed-plate, but will live on at Guildford; and Standard 2-6-4T No. 80138 had its insides put back and was sent to Bournemouth. 30;1

Plate 205: **75E THREE BRIDGES** The blizzard has obviously passed this way! N Class No. 31410 appears to be ducking between her blinkers – to get out of the cold? 31st December 1961.   31;2

Plate 206: **81A OLD OAK COMMON**
Standing fifth in the allocation league table
in the early 1950s, Old Oak, so close to
Willesden, was a must. Engines seemed to
be everywhere – here, 'Castle' 4-6-0 No.
5014 *Goodrich Castle* stands with 'Hall'
No. 7921 *Edstone Hall* at the side of one
part of the shed, on 29th April 1962.
197;*1L*

Plate 207: **81C SOUTHALL** Thankfully,
due to the preservation movement,
Southall has not been obliterated – so,
something similar to this scene could be
recreated. Unidentified '6100' Class
2-6-2T shows the effect of the later days
of GW steam – she is still in steam, but all
her numbers have gone! February
1965.   73;*3*

Plate 208: **81E DIDCOT** Preservation of this shed has gone further and something similar to this is still possible. On 14th October 1964, eight months before the shed closed to steam, the atmosphere is quite healthy, with a beautifully clean 'Hall' No. 4959 *Purley Hall* standing proudly in the yard. 47:1

Plate 209: **81F OXFORD** Standard '9F' No. 92220 *Evening Star* has always been a special engine; here she stands, just another engine on shed, at Oxford on 28th April 1963.   56;*1*

Plates 210 & 211: **82C SWINDON** Two views inside one of the Swindon roundhouses. **(Right):** Monopolizing the turntable, this is rather like a tank's convention! Left to right, are: Nos. 1658, 3652, 9721, 3684, 4612 and 4644. 9th April 1961. 127;*2.* **(Below):** This time in solitary confinement, '6100' Class No. 6161 contemplates the future. Ex-works on 20th October 1963, she lived another two years.   *1*

Plate 212: **82E BRISTOL (BARROW ROAD)** In normal working days, photographs of prototype Standard '9F' 2-10-0 No. 92000 were rare. In typical grime, she stands ready for her next duty, on shed on 6th December 1964.   56;*3*

Plate 213: **82F BATH (GREEN PARK)** Closed in 1966, in line with the rest of the S & D line, Green Park was a very attractive shed to visit, with its stonework and delightful engines. In the late evening sunshine of 8th April 1962, Standard 3 2-6-2T No. 82004 is enhanced by the glow. To the left No. 73052 also enjoys the sun. 51:2

Plate 214: **83B TAUNTON** Evidence of recent rain can be seen, in this general view of the shed yard, on 15th September 1962.   58;2

Plate 215: **83C EXETER** The day after the above, on 16th September 1962, and the sun shines brightly. '2800' Class 2-8-0 No. 2895 looks ex-works, as she stands simmering in the yard. 35:2

Plate 216: **83D LAIRA (PLYMOUTH)** One of the joys of visiting Laira, was to see the diminutive '1361' Class 0-6-0ST. Here, class member No. 1363 stands on the coal ramp, on 20th August 1961.   108;*1*

Plate 217: **83G PENZANCE** The end of the line, in Cornwall, engines were serviced here, before working back north. The shed's allocation was mainly express engines, with a few local passenger locos. Here, on 24th August 1961, original 'Grange' No. 6800 *Arlington Grange* stands by the coaler, with the shed buildings in the background.   30;*1*

Plate 218: **84A WOLVERHAMPTON (STAFFORD ROAD)** Once a thriving shed, by the time of this photograph on 1st December 1962, it had all but ceased its usefulness. Making a forlorn picture, are stored Kings – from front to back: Nos. 5022 *King Edward III,* 6015 *King Richard III,* 6014 *King Henry VII,* 6012 *King Edward VI* and 6017 *King Edward IV.* 66:1

Plate 219: **84B OXLEY** High up, on an embankment, overlooking the Race Course, Oxley was often a cold and windy place to visit. The foliage is lush enough, but needs attention, as 'Hall' No. 7917 *North Aston Hall,* without number or name, stands quietly. 25th July 1965. 67;*1*

Plate 220: **84C BANBURY** In steam days, this was a common and typical sight. Now, sadly, just a memory – this time from February 1965. 70;*3*

Plate 221: **84E TYSELEY** Another shed saved by preservation, it was part of the Birmingham District, which, in late steam days, delighted in stencilling numbers on engines! '5100' Class 2-6-2T No. 4168 has been treated thus, as has '5600' Class No. 5658 at the back. Sister engine No. 5606 is sandwiched between the two, on 25th July 1965.   118;1

Plate 222: **85A WORCESTER** Two views of 'Castle' No. 7025 *Sudeley Castle* standing over the ash pit, on 12th July 1964. Seen from inside the shed, with '6100' Class No. 6155 to the left.   *87:1*

Plate 223: The view this time, from the main line passing the shed. 3

Plates 224 & 225: **85B GLOUCESTER (HORTON ROAD) Top:** By the look of 'Austerity' No. 90040 and the shadows, 23rd June 1963 looks a fine summer's day. **Below:** In contrast, less than a month later, on 14th July, there is a deceptively cold wind, as can be seen from the exhausts of 'Castle' No. 7034 *Ince Castle* and 'Hall' No. 5914 *Ripon Hall!*   101;1 (Both)

Plate 226: **86A NEWPORT (EBBW JUNCTION)** With the heavy steel and coal trains and passengers radiating north, Newport had a perhaps surprisingly large allocation. Named engines were mostly visitors, however, as here in 1964, when 'Hall' No. 7909 *Heveningham Hall* was the guest. 143;*3*

Plate 227: **86A NEWPORT (EBBW JUNCTION)** Small tank engines were common, but by 4th September 1964 whilst '5700' Class No. 3747 takes water, diesels are making their mark!   *1*

Plate 228: **86C HEREFORD** Hereford's allocation was smal and medium engines; of the latter, '2251' Class 0-6-0 No. 2242 stands alone outside the shed building that closed four months later. 12th July 1964.   53:1

Plate 229: **86E SEVERN TUNNEL JUNCTION** Near the tunnel mouth, the shed was always a source of interest. Here, '5700' Class 0-6-0PT No. 4671 valiantly earns her crust, shunting '5100' Class No. 4156 and '7200' Class No. 7240 around the yard. 4th September 1964.   74;1

Plate 230: **86G PONTYPOOL RCAD** The Welsh hills can be seen in the background of a scene that has since changed drastically. On 1st September 1964, 7200' Class 2-8-2T No. 7233 potters about the shed yards, in brilliant sunshine.   *89:1*

Plate 231: **87C DANYGRAIG** To the normal spotter, Danygraig was one of those sheds not visited. On 2nd July 1963, it has seen better days, as has '5700' Class No. 6749, which is stored, having been withdrawn the previous October.   34;*1*

Plate 232: **87D SWANSEA EAST DOCK** Ex-Cardiff Railway 0-4-0ST No. 1338 saw sterling work in the dockyards of South Wales, finally working at Swansea. She is out of work here, on 2nd July 1963 and is not likely to work again, being withdrawn in September.   30;*1*

Plate 233: **88B RADYR** A new shed in the 1950s to serve Cardiff, it saw short service, being closed on 26th July 1965. '9400' Class tanks were domiciled here and No. 3405 can be seen, together with No. 9465, on 23rd June 1963.   Nil;*1*

Plate 234: **88C BARRY** Barry shed was passed by thousands, over the years, on their way to Butlins Holiday Camp on Barry Island. In the last month of service as a shed, it gives room to '2800' Class 2-8-0 No. 3848, on 2nd September 1964. 80;*1*

Plate 235: **88G LLANTRISANT** Long before the Royal Mint moved into town, two ex-GWR engines simmer quietly in the shed yard, on 1st September 1964. Left is '5700' Class No. 3612 and right '4200' Class No. 4285. The shed closed in October. 20;*1*

Plate 236: **88J ABERDARE** Tucked away in the Welsh valleys, Aberdare was a pleasing shed to visit. In 1950, its allocation was almost exclusively tanks and the picture looks no different on 1st September 1964. '4200' Class No. 5256 stands with '5700' 0-6-0 No. 3699 and sister engine No. 4278. 52;*1*

Plate 237: **88L CARDIFF EAST DOCK** Shed code apart, this is a time-less picture, even down to the appearance of the workman. Actually, the date is 4th September 1964 and '5600' Class No. 5601 is waiting for coal.   *62:1*

Plate 238: **89A SHREWSBURY** In 1950, the shed's allocation was half and half GW and MR and this mix stayed until the end of steam at the shed, in 1967. Here, MR 'Mogul' No. 46505 stands in classic style, on 14th July 1963, with 'Grange' No. 6845 *Paviland Grange* behind.   122;1

Plates 239 & 240: Finally, a look at Steam On Shed – Preserved Style. The place is Didcot and, showing how successful the GWS has been in recreating steam shed days, these photographs are almost timeless. They were actually taken on 5th June 1983.   1